MW00533305

Therapon is an exquisi... [by] Dan Beachy-Quick and Bruce Bond, a continuous thread of poems that defy any attempt at knowing who wrote what. *Therapon* is a journey, a song, a looping narrative, an exploration into spirit and word, and it exposes all our failures to find peace and redemption. Etymologically, "therapon" means "chamber" in Ancient Greek. It also means a person whose job/role is an attendant, a companion of lower rank, an aid, a slave, a servant who has committed (or was committed) to be willing to sacrifice all for a human master or supernatural deity. One thinks of *The Iliad*, one thinks of the global history of slavery, and one thinks of how horribly religion and dogma have failed us, and how fiercely the yearning for a spiritual life lives on. One thinks of how "therapy" derives, also, from the roots of "therapon," and then one becomes very sad, and a bit bemused. *Therapon* is also an examination of how language is inadequate to the human and the human spirit. A mature, serious work, *Therapon* reminds us that humans are beasts capable of immense violence. Why can't we evolve? And yet, like the animals, we also love, we also seek.

Gillian Conoley

T H E R A P ° N

BRUCE BOND   DAN BEACHY-QUICK

Tupelo Press
North Adams, Massachusetts

Therapon
Copyright © 2023 Dan Beachy-Quick and Bruce Bond. All rights reserved.

ISBN-13: 978-1-946482-99-0 (paperback)
ISBN-13: 978-1-961209-03-9 (eBook)

Epigraph from *Totality and Infinity* by Emmanuel Levinas, translated
by Alphonso Lingis. Duquesne University Press, 1969. Reproduced
with permission.

Library of Congress Control Number: 2023028709
Cataloging-in-Publication record available from the Library of Congress.

Cover and text design by Kenji Liu.
Cover art: Mike + Doug Starn, STRUCTURE OF THOUGHT 5. © 2023
Mike and Doug Starn / Artists Rights Society (ARS), New York Used
by permission.

First paperback edition December 2023

All rights reserved. Other than brief excerpts for reviews and
commentaries, no part of this book may be reproduced by any means
without permission of the publisher. Please address requests for reprint
permission or for course-adoption discounts to:

Tupelo Press
P.O. Box 1767
North Adams, Massachusetts 01247
(413) 664-9611 / Fax: (413) 664-9711
editor@tupelopress.org / www.tupelopress.org

Tupelo Press is an award-winning independent literary press that
publishes fine fiction, non-fiction, and poetry in books that are a joy
to hold as well as read. Tupelo Press is a registered 501(c)(3) nonprofit
organization, and we rely on public support to carry out our mission
of publishing extraordinary work that may be outside the realm of the
large commercial publishers. Financial donations are welcome and are
tax deductible.

Language is not enacted within a consciousness; it comes to me from the Other and reverberates by putting it in question.

—EMMANUEL LEVINAS

I.

1:

count to one   it is as far into infinity
as you can go   far as the hermit in his cave

—:o

Far as the wall whose edifice mirrors no one here
though a torch might float a shadow   across a herd
drawn in blood   minerals berries   char   unctuous
with resins of the myrtle   it took a cave to pull these
horses out   to lay a silhouette untraced   unnamed
that came later if at all long   after the kill   the bison
the blood   that binds   reminds you   two came first
the mother of one   you were no one with your crayons
once and lay inside a sterile tent   what did you know
of the fever that turns a smile yellow   flesh a stranger
the sun behind the curtain was in you all along   the sun
the crayon the slaughtered beast of dawn   *you* I say
and a million figured horses thunder through the room

:1

Against the mind-wall, the mirror-mind
there the herd of shadows grazes still
those berries in the blood, memories, forms
a finger plowed into rock, mulberry, blood,
myrtle, each one gives a shadow a mind,
a shadow a mouth, unnames what it names,
bison, bird-headed staff, horse, headdress,
you have no mother, child, only memory
that fever in the cave you thought to cure
by swallowing strange ink and spitting it out,
your hand pressed against the wall, knowledge
is what that is called, among the slaughtered herds, you,
your hand's silhouette, blank beast, the other beasts make room

2:

If you want this room a little larger   try a mirror
try a word   touch the wall   of a dressing room whose
faces graze the glass   my first memory is a meadow
like this   a beast in the window that has no other side
mind you   I was no one   and then my shadow
followed   names, names   they fell into the mouths
of those I loved   bird, bison   the talking horse inside
my black and white TV   my mother taught me   this
is this   or close enough   and words cured a loneliness
I did not know   until I gave to it   a name   stranger
still   I named a mirror   and it turned   into a wall   I
named a beast   and in   that moment a herd arrived
you understand   you as   you   the only   ness   of two

:2

Between gold and forgetting, a shadow
hides its face, shyness of the child
behind his mother's dress, but memory
is the only mother he has, bloodless
but warm, welcoming you to become no one,
too   Like a coin you carry in your mouth a name
this coin, this mother of exchange, what
new loneliness will it buy?   A way to cross
where the river shallows   Stranger, cross
the river   Put away your face, become a mirror
Do you see the herd crossing the meadow?
Yes, that's your mother   The herd that calls you you

3:

In a dark time I make a sack out of my shadow
and crawl inside   I curl into its balm   its palm
its womb   what is death   I asked my mother
once   then a silence   that grew more silent still
and still   I bleed pure light   into a summer dress
its roses blushed   transfused   unpetalled down
the lineage of small encounters   when I got hurt
my mother closed the wound   with her lips   she
plucked a coin   from my eye   placed it in a sack
for the ferry   my shadow   hers   they made one
shadow once   here   at the entrance to the park
at dawn   one black tower felled across the river
Kaw   Kaw she said   and then the word was gone

:3

"Meet your shadow" my mother said, pointing
at me. My palm opened all by itself. Nothing
in me said "Open." I had asked the questions
I knew to ask, and waited for silence to tell me
what to do. Death waited patiently. Light came
down the infinite stairs wearing a summer dress—
the beauty hurt me. I don't know how else to say it.
"Meet your wound," my mother said, pointing
at me. A coin fell out of my eye, why?
I wasn't crying. The ferryman holds out his hand
in what is always the entrance to the present tense.
Dawn's black river. "Meet your fallen tower,"
my mother said. The crow looked, called, flew away.

4:

The end of the story is a car   abandoned by the Golden Gate
but once in the black pool that drowned the hours   alive
there was no end   there was a man who brooded over the keys
his baby grand afloat the water   a whisper without caller or called
I   want to say the wound goes deeper   each end has another
let death wait   we have other pressing matters   ask the cry
that brought us into the world   ask the tiny circle inside us all
where none of it matters   but still   you cry   you play your love
ballad to an empty room   rings of smoke blow over the sands
of the Presidio   black bile runs in a keyboard's hands   surprise
remember the bus north of harbor   how it stopped in the woods
to let the black bear cross   and everyone looked at each other
you me crow bear   powerless and still   before the eyes of strangers

:4

The poem creates the distance it must cross? Yes, it does.
Makes itself a bridge above the dark hours? Yes.
And you're telling me that broken water rises? I am.
And some pleasure whispers on the surface? That's right.
A wound works its way through me, mouth to anus? It's true.
Matter teaches me to sing by singing in the emptiness. Yes, it does.
The world is a circle inside us all? So it's been said.
The poem creates a circle around all it loves? Yes.
But leaves me out, smoke in an empty room? That's right.
Black bile turns the soul melancholy? According to the books.
I don't remember reading any books. You've read many.
I remember a black bear standing up by the side of the road. Yes.
And a bridge across which all grew stranger. Yes, stranger. That's
        this bridge.

5:

A stranger walks into a bar   and the bartender asks
the usual?   happens all the time   but today the TV
is on fire   and then an ad   whose medicated sadness
walks   into a pasture   oblivious to the possible
side effects   one of whom is death   which feels more
like a central feature   but today   a crippled willow
pours a little river   through the wound   of the eye
whatever the lie   it keep breaking   out   of a circle
as worlds do in poems   violence in cartoons   and you
dear sadness   I want to ask   are you wearing a mask
are you safe   I need you   the way an actor needs an act
of faith   and then a curtain   and sometimes the tears
continue   long after   never knowing whom we mourn

:5

The bartender tells his favorite joke—
A man walks into a bar, time walks in
To a man, fire walks in offering medicine
Called *Pastura*, the "possible" is the only
Side-effect, death walks into a bar
Paying for drinks with rhyme, a willow
Wallows in self-pity in the corner, eyes echo
Wounds, some ghosts play bridge, a mouth
Says *O*, and the circle expands, larger
Than the world, a mask walks into a bar
Looking for a face, any face will do, need
Walks into a bar searching for lost faith,
Faith says "happily ever after," and in walks you.

6:

Imagine a line against the dry horizon   call it
Pastura   call it south of the Sangre de Christos
a watering hole for locomotives   who bear
letters for a post that lo appears ex nihilo a chapel
a bar   a makeshift cross among the nameless
crosses of a field   say the word and I am there
says the word   and then by railcar a little news
and no this is no pasture soaked in blood we are
not angels   if you are not sure   ask a neighbor
ask the choired zeros ever wider than the walls
or the ropes of smoke that disappear and ghost
the rise   and fall of towns   in waves   ask those
who linger after   whose tumblers runneth over

:6

Eden is only some letters buried in a pasture,
Grass obedient to an inner law
Also commanding us, water inside a bone
No one can drink. The mind works its *if-then*
Logic, builds from nothing the architecture of *is*,
But the middle is excluded, the little hinge
Of the hyphen, that hidden ampersand, barren
For some, for others, the only form of prayer
God heeds. The dead speak in grammar of paradise—
No breath so no vowels, no pause between words, ask
Any question and the answer sounds the same, choir
Of twigs cracking as they burn, a song not of blame
Or knowledge, but something else, what *runneth* within & away.

7:

Music   yes   it runs away   from what   I ask
an inner law   a world   a witness   looking back
who whispers   you   fire runs away from earth
and fire   Eden runs from the words   *Eden*
law   the vowels   of paradise are letters after
all   and so   dear Eden   I am writing you about
a friend   he loved you   more   are you listening
friend   I do not think so   but I am one child
of fire   and the music here is beautiful   never
true   or false   profound   yes   but never wise
I run away   from home   and only later   the lotus
eaters   of the pasture crumple   and fade   I am
no believer   and ache   pure light   as Eden must

:7

Music took the single thread and tangled it
Into a knot called mind. I didn't witness
What happened inside me—thought, earth
Fire. Music took the wood and planed two doors
And sang them the law of hinges. I didn't make
Myself the gates of paradise I am writing about,
I only walked through them. Listen, friend—
A child strikes matches in the dust, dips crickets
In kerosene, sets them on fire. What is beautiful
Isn't true or false. "Yes" has no mouth, but speaks
Its wisdom in us. Yes, there is no home.
Yes, you can eat the grass in the pasture
But it will not save you. Yes, you cannot eat light.

8:

A childhood friend told me she was   saved
and I could be if I wanted   and thus the news
I am in danger   in every canto of the word
saved   I heard   not angels   but the monster
music in films I loved   where the subcortex
of a cloud speaks the language of the animals
so I placed the word *saved*   on a breath I blew it
through a door that yawned   I saw not angels
but a friend   who died   and then she held out
a hand that turned to fire fury cloud   I cannot
eat light   alone   though I see the sun in every
meal   the burning friend   in every visible thing

:8

A friend told me I was acting like a child.
The friend was my wife. The news
Came as no surprise. The dangerous words
I kept inside me, a monster with an angel
In his mouth. I love the taste of clouds
And angels taste like clouds, the endless animal-
Shapes of clouds, none of which breathe,
But ride on breath, west to east, those angels
Graze the morning meadows. My anger died
Again. Like a child I opened my hand.
I wanted something to eat. The sun gave me light.
A meal for the invisible thing inside me.

9:

Every angel is a monster   a woman says
it breaks a natural law   she tells   a ghost
at the dinosaur museum   where birds fly
through revolving doors   each cry as brief
as the stars   that halo   a blow to the head
every winged thing   the street spoons in
through the mouths of halls suffers hunger
dread   the rock below the rock   of anger
I see it   in their eyes   every bead a museum
every dawn   a janitor sweeps another hour
back into the night it came from   but once
here I heard a woman's voice   here it comes
she said   open wide   before I can remember

:9

An angel walks the museum hall holding a spoon
Full of cough syrup. The Law is sick again—
Law of the dinosaur hidden now in the bird,
Law of the door that is, at the same time, both
Open & closed. The door that is Time. The stars
Obey the grave edicts. The broken pair of wings
The child wore daily for a year, suffering her desire
To fly, thrown down in anger among the rocks
And litter—the wings also obey. I see the same
Law sick inside myself. Every day, for an hour,
I keep my mouth open. One night it will happen.
A voice will arrive. The voice will carry a spoon
& the medicine will heal what's in me. I remember—

10:

Wherever a law a criminal says a book I love
and then a rival enters the conversation
and sucks the laughter from a child in the hall
laws are the bones of rituals   they skeleton
our jails he says and a memory of my therapist
replies   some folks need to be tightened
some loosened   some angels fly through prison
walls to give instructions to the killer who
feels absolved and maybe it is a little   soon
or late I do know this somedays my great
mistakes return like breath after the verdict
like rivers pulled out of the sea then I let them
go I try I cast them to the sobbing of the deep

:10

Some books I love as I love my children.
In the midst of a conversation I remember
A sentence that—like the child walking home
From school, reciting the names of bones—
Steps suddenly into the room, and says:
It is very unhappy, folks, this discovery we've made,
But too late to be helped, that we exist. A loose angel
Is called obtuse. What is a right angel? The instructions
Bewilder some, absolve a little. I'm guilty,
I know. Somedays I dog-ear the corner of
My child to read later when it's easier to breathe;
Then kiss the book goodnight and tuck it in the sea.
& then one is sobbing, which one? *I don't want to go to sleep.*

II.

10:

The discovery that one exists is to the child
called the Fall of Man Once we lived in what we saw
says the child in a book I too love these words
and so I come to them to you with questions
who open like eyes believer and skeptic alike
come in we are all of us fallen from the world
says the book whose doors close up the room
of sleeping children and still the words remain
they blossom in the dark is there any other way
to live but fallen therefore haunted alone born
to question go on ask your books your hand
your friend where does the lost companion end
what fallen heaven jewels the morning grass

:10

...heedful retreat in the face of being is a sentence
I love in a book I find confusing. But I love
To be confused. Or, I mean, I don't mind it—
Having a mind. The same author writes
About thinking as wild deer grazing in meadow.
A child points at them as they leap away—
The child, a thinker; the deer, the thoughts.
In another book I love, a man is so angry
The word for his anger only describes wrath
The gods feel. The only song in the book
Is the song he sings, sitting by his boat.
He weeps by the sea calling out for his mother.
I know that song. Who isn't a child of the deep.

9:

Some questions talk softly to themselves
as answers do when lonely and confused
are we so different you and I the answer
says and the ocean slides a whisper in as
oceans do it sighs the sigh of the worried
on the couch talking to a therapist behind
us in the dark I have a friend a therapist
who tells me the misinformed are the most
resolute so *certain* she whispers children
of the deep are everywhere words words
and the stones they lie on I was grazing in
the fields all day and I smelled the earth as
it burned you there can you smell it are you sure

:9

What is true? I keep forgetting. The first
Therapist was the angel talking to the man,
Or the man talking to the angel? The one
Who knows the cosmic eros and repeats
The patterns, or the one who knows nothing
But prunes the peonies back in paradise.
Paradise? I keep forgetting if it's true.
If knowledge is good or bad or just a stomach
Suffering indigestion. God a kind of gossip.
Lust is what? Some line pointing out my body
To what my body wants? & the mind—stop it.
I know. The mind a museum. Standing in front
Of the display where I think about the display.

8:

That last thing you said   there was a question
standing just in back of it   and behind that
another question   how many angels can you
fit on the prick of the needle   questions feel
that essential   small in the context of earth
whose biosphere breathes a little bit of everywhere
and yes   me too   I stood before that counter
a step away from whomever   spoke   as me
my hope for my child is the restlessness that makes
an art of seeing   I have known a bitter fact
that ate a family   because they called it a story
among stories   they ate the fact   unaware   teeth
bright   knives crossed   they carved the beast together

:8

My mother taught me about our faith
Seldom practiced. We believe in no hell,
She said, but there is a heaven. One day I was
A child in the underground parking garage
Of *Cinderella City Mall*. She looked at me.
This is hell, she said, not meaning the mall.
I remember I loved most the magic shop.
I rubbed my fingers together and smoke
Rose in wisps. I bought itching powder
& dumped it down my back. It didn't itch.
It burned. Lit match-tips or sparks from fire
Within. The harm I do to myself as a joke
Hurts most. What do I know about salvation?

7:

What do I know   I wanted to say
the word I raised above the others
but she was sick and afraid and full
of questions   the kind a child asks
what is death   where is uncle Bob
and when I was a child   and Bob
a liar and a drunk   my mother said
a better place   I always loved that trick
how he pulled a quarter from my ear
I was looking at the one hand and poof
a little silver in the other   my head
must be full of coins   out of nowhere
I thought of that   of him   who was I to know

:7

Fire steers all things; or is it lightning?
It depends on the translation as so much depends.
The ancient mystics saw each black letter
As a flame, and so I've learned to read
By the dark light of the letters themselves.
True vision, they say, is as lightning at night—
A stuttering flash so sudden so bright
Seeing is what happens after the revelation
Of sight. The *alpha-bet* recites itself from *a* to *z*
& *z* to *a* simultaneously forever & that is
Either the name or the definition of God—
I don't remember which, it depends on your position
As so much depends. Fire first. Fire last. Lightning flash.

6:

So tell me   what do you see   the therapist asked
the woman   who gazed at a watermark overhead
a Rorschach of rain   in the shape of a head   half
eaten by time   the shape of the letter *a*   or is it *d*
after a fire   the sizzle of rain   that turns to letters
she burned   when the marriage was over   to think
a word could crown a candle   as once believed
and what is fire if not   the face   of light   pushed
through the older younger   or pulled like flowers
through the eyes of stems   or a January   garden
through the flower   whose voices are these that fall
like stars   muttering the alphabet forward and back
pacing the floor   waiting for some god to answer

:6

Nothing comes of nothing a different no-
Thing than the first, a kind of ground, a
Burial mound, loose dirt the hand gropes
Into a pile, or a finger draws a circle,
The emptiness that wasn't there now is there,
Soul's primer, the letter *aleph*, solitary
Teacher who makes no sound, love and be
Silent, is that the lesson, or is the lonely student,
The letter *bet*, who is so afraid he builds
A box and climbs inside, and from within, says
Fear is a home—. So is the pasture. So is the
Past. Say a word and I am there. Some self
That says I with me, or for me, therapist, field.

5:

I ask my cat if he knows the difference
between a figure and a ground and he
says nothing yet a different nothing
than the one that circled me when he
was alive and could not eat but today
his eyes and the sky that tumbles in
look hungry eager to be included so
yes he knows the difference between
nothing and me and nothing of his
knowing when out of nowhere I call
a name that means less than the voice
that calls the bowl I fill I do not think
he sees his face afloat the circle the one
he kneels to drink until it is not there

:5

Dug a pitkin and poured in the blood
But no ghosts arrived, not even a rumor
In a forgotten mouth, the war.
Baked an oat-cake in the fire-pit
And put it in the table, but the clouds
Passed by, never stepping down,
In translucent gown, from the sky.
The violence kept playing on the screen inside.
The cat sat on my lap or bit the cuff of my hand.
Ads for medicine broke the explosive tedium:
Lyrica, Moderna, Levitra, Asprin, Viagra, Suspira.
I went back outside and mixed the wine & water.
The rain fell from the cloud but never hit the ground.

4:

And what could be more fortunate   given
the choices rain must have   to be or to be
the ache   that lingers in the phantom vessel
you are not alone   meet me   on the stairs
of our ghost   arrangements *Viagra Niagara*
Suspira   whatever else goes   with wine   sad
as your news   how beautiful of you to bear it
I have seen a cloud twist into an eye   afloat
the earth   alders tore their garments   rocks
of ice flew sideways   out of the approaching
margin   I was staring through a pair of doors
nothing but glass between me and the terrible
marvel   some yards north   one moment   long ago

:4

The messenger comes and says there is a wound.
There is a wound and there is music. There is
An abandoned car by a bridge. There is music.
There is a mule whose eyes deny the stranger's
Philosophy. There is a piano. There is a reminder
Of a day long ago playing scales for an eternal
Hour in the middle C of the dove's call. & a cloud
Of gnats above the water each body a point
In the endless geometric proof writing itself
Before our eyes—the geometry of the wound.
It is everywhere and nowhere. The wound wanders.
It moves through the world as if the world weren't
There. The messenger points at you, then the moon.

3:

Say this is   a pane of glass that turns into a mirror
at certain angles   the way a fish turns   the image
disappears   and in its place   a face cut from another
order of being   there   one sea surges out of the
sea   it wanders   at night   a little farther from shore
the other grows warmer   every year   one day it will
lay its weeds at my door   to every sea   the million
small decisions of the deep   the new   whose science
has not yet been invented   one day a soul tears its flame
from the architecture   it chills the glasses in the room
if one were the sum of their choices   whose waves
are these   that close   in us   their eyes   whose fish
turn to the face and back   to who they think   they are

:3

The dark inside the dark my daughter said
Is what she is afraid of is why she will not
Go to sleep. Easy to turn off the lamp
In the room so each corner fills with night.
But why make another night inside yourself
By closing your eyes. A darker night.
& then again as before there is the river
To cross, swollen by memory and by rain,
& the breeze of your mother's voice
Saying you are not alone even when you know
You are alone. & then the palm tree
Of the far shore. & the owl nesting in the fronds.
A mistaken thought about beauty & death.

2:

Blooms in jars   tell you   earth is somewhere
far away   death   finds another word
to wear   a black to bind   the mirrors
at the party   it is just   that personal
someone reads   a song full of black
birds at the end   another shoreline eats
the shore   that is no end   we know
say   one steps into a boat   that sways
its cradle on the fog   *soul*   from *saiwalo*
ancient Norse   for *sea*   my first word
had a face   and when the face left   it
took that word   the one I heard   the one
I chased with every word   thereafter

:2

Is is the path I want to be on, where thinking thinks
and is not thought, where saying says but is not said.
I read about the nature of thinking & also I looked.
A man sits on a stone, head on hand, & his fingers
bend backward toward his throat. A gesture of
mourning says a footnote, an asterisk, a star. Or is it
the thinker points at what departs? The herd wary
& the grass wet with morning. & then there is the fear
you feel when an animal fears you, & you want to run
away from yourself. & words then seem to speak
inside you what you could you never tell yourself—
memory is your mother, and she says one word: *was*.
Mirror-self of the 2nd person. You suck your thumb.

1:

The I that is and the I that was   are sitting on the edge
of the wilderness   inching toward the end   how great
to drink with images   on mute overhead   where news
is   never   new   these outlines   host a flock   of souls
to whom I owe the world   but I too fear the schoolyard
stairwell   to my former terrors   call them words   these
animals who growl at the mirror   I think   the universe
swells and breaks our ribs   so we might crawl out   alive
the mirror tells you   our map of islands   lesions   nation
after nation   sinks into the vellum   but I see boundaries
still   names of rivers   gone dry   the silence of a stranger
I am not yet   the lust in luster   the steam   in the breath
the throated O that is not personal   I hear it everywhere

:1

The flower is so beautiful you have to draw it
On a page, & the bison so beautiful, & the bird-
Headed man, & the outline of your own hand—
So beautiful you have to draw it. The blind singer
Understands. There in the half-lit after-life grove
Sitting in his folding chair, reciting the ABC's
To the children who are not there. A brick is
A block of ice; a pyramid is a pillar of snow.
Do plants have a soul? Yes or no. Do stones?
The philosopher sat inside his own shadow.
He said justice is a perfect cube. In the world
Nowhere, not among pinecones or pinwheels,
Is such a cube. You must draw it. Here's a cave wall.

III.

1:

An act of kindness is beautiful   although the form
is formless or rather it overflows the cup it was   it
says to the square take heart we need you   we need
a steady hand at the bed of the slaughtered couple
to measure   to note   I have known many charities
who stepped into a square and broke and breaking
was no gift   the souls were gone   I too have wept
on a bluff above the gather and surge of Monteverdi
because a friend had fallen in   I lacked the clear eye
of squares   but my ear was a deeper matter   I loved
the symmetry of pillars   the home key at either gate
and leaving I felt better   being lost beyond the vines
across the iron   that called me to the woods ahead...

:1

...."Justice is a perfect cube." Aristotle said it.
A boy I spent summers roaming the woods
My ancestors roamed, above the fallen-down
Mill, now the local swim-hole, a waterfall
You could dive underneath and breathe in
A cave behind the ever-shattering, never-broken
Window and look out, seeing nothing just—
Just light filling a surface; the same woods edged
The cemetery my ancestors are buried in,
Graveyard we own and that owns us, the *Quick*
Cemetery, it's true. I picked up the pine-cones
From trees my great-grandfather planted. I
Put flags behind the veteran stones. Not one...

2:

...flag but half a dozen of one nation so singular
they made a foreigner of each the fish of our colors
in the wind ever-fluttering never moving on if
justice is a square God a circle the silence of God
is a grave inside a circle in a square my wife was
a beaten child in her sleep she cries out still you
are safe I say and if she hears we are none the wiser
the story of the story ends the square of the room
has a hole no wall can close no fair reprisal no
school of stars and banners sublimates a cry like that
no stone can seal the gash in earth it is the gash
there will be days she lies in bed still as a waterfall
with a cave inside a blush of light across the surface...

:2

...but many of my own kin buried there—
my grandfather, crippled by polio, who fished
the crick by holding his rod out the pick-up's
open window, who knew the names of the dead
he buried, is buried himself there, ashes in a box.
& cousin Lettie who jumped from the train
as it entered a tunnel, going to New York City
to see the unveiling of the *Statue of Liberty*.
Time darkened the photo we found in the attic
but there she was, as once she was, staring
through her face at me, accusing me of being
alive when she is not. What is the grass? a child
asked. It is what grows around the stones. It is...

3:

...a scripture   where every word is different   from
the others   there is a word for that   a singular blade
little wonder   the end of each expects a story   and
sometimes   there is none   the untold life   is   here
and there   a song whose music is a boat on the river
whose face dissolves   I come at night to float   one
ghost among the others   who descended into heaven
through a gate   whose graven meadow   lays down
the path ahead or one such path   I find comfort in a
field because it does not care   so alone you disappear
like a father   a woman waves her kerchief at a statue
her harbor radiant as knives   the story is yours the part
that never happened   the untold loss is everywhere...

:3

...the endless chores, gas-powered weed-whacker's
cicada drone, the ditch so overgrown hours died
by the sickle that could have been wasted in dreams,
the John Deere tractor skirting the red currants
and the edge of the woods where the scarlet tanager
darted into darkness, a last thought or a lost one,
I felt it, the thing, that *thing*, what could be known
that I would never know, it was against the law
what I wanted, to let the grass grow, leaf-out
& drop its seed, for the graveyard stones to be
buried in the green flood of a rising sea, the wind
making its waves, death's whole fact as gentle as
the grass bent down where all night the doe lay...

4:

...alive or dead I cannot say   I have seen a web
cloud a pair of nostrils   the doe's eye   jeweled
with flies   unafraid   the grave of suns that fell
and just kept falling   my mother   my mother's
mother   the volt that arced her spine on the table
they lit my helmet in the woods   who has not drunk
from the river   and looking up   forgot the trail
that led here   though a vague uncertain sorrow
lingers   and then another and my word for that is
music   when my mother could not sleep I brought
her a radio   for every clarity the song withheld   it
gave permission   the way a friend gives a mourner
space   a box of breath so abundant   it overflows...

:4

...that emptiness the body leaves behind it
after it has wandered off, the storage shed,
the frontal cortex, the heart's hidden chamber
where the phantasms all together play
solitaire, the open hand, the words etched
on stones, a name and a date of birth and death,
the emptiness a name becomes, the sayable
nothing a name is as it echoes out
through the infinite non-place where time
has no rule... shaggy pines and huckleberry,
butter-cup and peony, let the things I save
save me. I remember you, you map of the
world framed on the dining room wall...

5:

...you whose waters never breathe   whose
names of coastal cities float across the harbor
save me says a tiny island in the South Pacific
that is   no longer there   every map   one face
across another   save me says a ring my father
left behind and so I slip it on   so large it falls
like an angel   every fetish a mask whose holes
await the living eye   who alive is not a child
of the objects in the room   save me they say
and then a little monster comes to your door
you give her sweets   as is the custom   when
death calls   you feign surprise   empty your fist
into her bag   a white slip designed for a pillow...

:5

...a white veil caught in the apple-tree; no son,
the apple-tree is on fire; no, father, the apple-
tree is blooming; no, son, the wind tangled
a grocery store bag in the branches; no, father,
the white tatter of a skunk's stripe flew off
through the air like a bandage searching
for a wound; no, son, no. My father never
called me son; I never called him father.
The farther away I get from childhood, the more
the oracle of the side-view mirror chants
its endless truth: objects in the mirror are closer
than they appear. The bee is deep inside the
peony, but so is the beetle. The old barn speaks...

6:

...the old door opens and the words are flies
bits of hay   voices of a father who has lost
his tongue   and the back and forth continues
no I say   and silence echoes   the apple tree
litters the lawn with petals and grasses welter
when I was young I was a monster   I loved
beauty just that much   I burst into an aureole
of peonies and bees   I was just that scared   I
placed a cube inside a song and called it *barn*
or *justice* or *the American conflict in southeast Asia*
I was just that damaged   I said look   father
and he said   nothing   though today I saw him
in the mirror   listening closer than he appeared...

:6

...to gesture to the attic, to gesture holding
the barrel of a rifle and cocking the hammer,
to gesture the pulling of the trigger, staggering
back at the recoil, then turned the scene around,
my father did in this memory-dream, got down
on all fours, grew a tail, black fur with white stripe,
he gorged in the garden, the peas, the carrots,
took the bait in the trap, cowered when the
cage-door clapped shut, seemed to, seemed to
look at me in bewilderment, seemed to ask me
how did this happen, did you do this, can you
let me out, what can I give you to let me out
of this cage, dream of the cage, metaphor of
the cage, asking me, his child, to fetch the gun...

7:

...to put a hole in the dream   morning
 cuts each eye   and pulls   a bullet   out
 and yet I see him still   the man in the cage
 how he whimpers at the door   he says
 you were a child once   and I took you
 to the slaughter house   where the pigs
 writhed on hooks that moved   on way
 to the man with a blade and one dull job
 you waited for the sun to cut   your eye
 and pull the image out   remember   or
 was it you who left the image   you who
 abandoned the night theater   in disrepair
 where cries on hooks dragged on and on...

:7

...a joke he loved, my grandfather, driving back
from the P&C with new meds in a white bag,
to pull the red pickup off the road by the ag school's
swine-yard where, in open pens, piglets suckled
on sows' teats, & the sheer pink girth seemed
a miracle, tufts of white fur on triangle ears.
"That's your real family," he'd say. Dark hog
by himself in the shade. "Back over there
are your second cousins, twice removed.
This is your great uncle, kicked out of church
for drinking." I laughed each time. I liked seeing
those pigs. I met them again in high school
& again as an adult. Circe's island. Elpenor...

8:

...hungover walked off a roof at dawn
 and broke his neck he taught me in death
 you can be two places at once your ghost
 in the underworld your flesh in a linen of flies
 island breezes you are not your suffering
 Alan Watts said and so I closed my eyes
 and waited for the ship to return I died
 in my sleep again and floated above my
 body as if it were a figure in a local fable
 with a head full of words pigs reflections
 on animal pain that make of it a creature
 in the world a child bathed in blood I was
 born the moment they cut me from another...

:8

...I carry the world a shield against memory
but every arrow pierces through—
pierces through, but slows, slows, so slow
the wound is almost a choice
I make. Or is it a choice made for me.
The barn with a sailboat inside it. Why
remember, of all things, that? Seagull white
in the darkness it kept a brooding glow
as if it had knowledge of something I would
never know. No sails, no mast. A secret
past no one cared about, or cared about enough
not to share. An arrow passes through the world
and becomes a boat. Strange wound, the mind...

9:

...a strange choice   the one I make   before
I know I make it   the plural of I is a boat
that glows   the white noise of a radio inside
the barn made the crackle of rain remember
I cannot tell you where that was   the green
lamp of the dial   the needle fixed on no one
station   every beam of earthly light is broken
one part wind   the other sail

                            I broke down once
and the Boulder River kept me   company
the plural of water was water   the love   I
lost became at last   what it was   what does
water know   of where a river starts

                                   where it ends
it is busy being water   which is to say   another...

:9

...I came late to the realization that all along
I'd been in the world. Like a chair
with an inner life. Like a map of the world
on a wall. I think I am pointing at something
I'm not—I am, but I'm not.

        Other realizations
came more slowly. Like the hole in the hickory
that pierces the tree through. Like that circle
of blue in the trunk of the tree.

           & that ghost
at work on the workbench in the attic, winter
radio playing the college game, hammering
shells into nuts, sealing the nuts in mason jars...
Realization that nothing ever touches, like...
I used to deride similes; then I became one...

10:

...I touch the air between me and the looking
glass   the way light touches air   on it journey
two came first   the mother of one   remember
therapon: to attend: :

                                   when the wind blew
the tree shook its hair   as if   a bee were there
and so I named the flower *bee*   the bee *flame*
that sips the stamen of the candle   I called
the cup of light   *therapon: to care for*   like
a surgeon over a hole

                         me here   my father far away
the day they laid in him a stranger's heart   gave
it a shock   one day a needle drags   a filament
that in time dissolves   like   a sun on its passage
years later when he died   he took with him a stranger...

:10

...a grief-substitute so different than a substitute
for grief. One finds comfort in keeping old calendars
on an attic shelf, a kind of instruction manual,
next to the volume *How to Use a Hammer
in Twelve Easy Steps*, next to the volume *Meaning
of a Stick*. The other takes the broken-rainbow-
waterfall-mist of another's memory and straps it
to ankles and to thighs, straps it around the midriff
where the soul sometimes sits, covers the shoulders
and forearms, but leaving the head bare, grabs
a hammer, or grabs a stick, and runs straight into
battle, letting his friend cry by the boat in the barn
for as long as he needs to cry. Which might be forever.
Or longer yet. There is no end to such therapy...

Acknowledgments

The authors would like to thank the editors of the following journals in which poems from this manuscript originally appeared: *Agni*, *col*, *Diode*, *The Laurel Review*, *Mississippi Review*, *Plume*, *Prairie Schooner*, *Sand Journal*, *Sugar House Review* and *Tupelo Quarterly*.

BRUCE BOND is the author of 35 books including, most recently, *Patmos* (Juniper Prize, UMass, 2021), *Behemoth* (New Criterion Prize, 2021), *Liberation of Dissonance* (Schaffner Award for Literature in Music, Schaffner, 2022), *Choreomania* (MadHat, 2023), and *Invention of the Wilderness* (LSU, 2023), plus two books of criticism, *Immanent Distance* (UMichigan, 2015) and *Plurality and the Poetics of Self* (Palgrave, 2019). Among his forthcoming books are *Vault* (Richard Snyder Award, Ashland) and *The Dove of the Morning News* (Test Site Poetry Prize, UNV).

DAN BEACHY-QUICK is a poet, essayist, and translator, whose recent books include translations of Sappho, *Wind—Mountain—Oak* (Tupelo 2023) and pre-Socratic philosophy, *The Thinking Root* (Milkweed Editions, Seedbank, 2023). Recent poetry incudes *Arrows* (Tupelo 2020) and *Variations on Dawn and Dusk* (Omnidawn 2019), long-listed for the National Book Award in Poetry. A critic of literary reverie, he has written monographs on Herman Melville's *Moby Dick* and the poetry and poetics of John Keats. His work has been supported by the Monfort, Lannan, and Guggenheim Foundations. He teaches at Colorado State University, where he is a University Distinguished Teaching Scholar.

RECENT AND SELECTED TITLES FROM TUPELO PRESS